A NOTE TO PARENTS ABOUT BEING GREEDY

Nothing upsets social balance as much as greed. When one person in a group takes more than his or her fair share, the entire group suffers the negative consequences.

The purpose of this book is to teach children how to determine what is a fair share. In addition, it helps children understand and embrace the importance of each person taking only his or her fair share.

Reading and discussing this book with your child can help him or her overcome the greed inherent in most young children who are not yet socialized. This will make it possible for your child to experience a greater level of success in most social situations.

Family life provides a perfect classroom for teaching children how to avoid being greedy. Begin by carefully providing the rationale for a fair share in each and every situation that requires sharing. Soon, your child will be able to determine for himself or herself what is a fair share. Reinforce non-greedy behavior by acknowledging and affirming your child every time he or she takes only a fair share.

This book belongs to:

Published by Scholastic Inc.
90 Old Sherman Turnpike, Danbury, CT 06816.

SCHOLASTIC and associated logos are trademarks and/or registered trademarks of Scholastic Inc.

ISBN 0-7172-8598-7

First Scholastic Printing, October 2005

A Book About
Being Greedy

by Joy Berry

SCHOLASTIC INC.

New York Toronto London Auckland Sydney
Mexico City New Delhi Hong Kong Buenos Aires

This book is about Randy and his friends T. J. and Tami.

Reading about Randy and his friends can help you understand and deal with **being greedy.**

Sometimes you need to share things with other people.

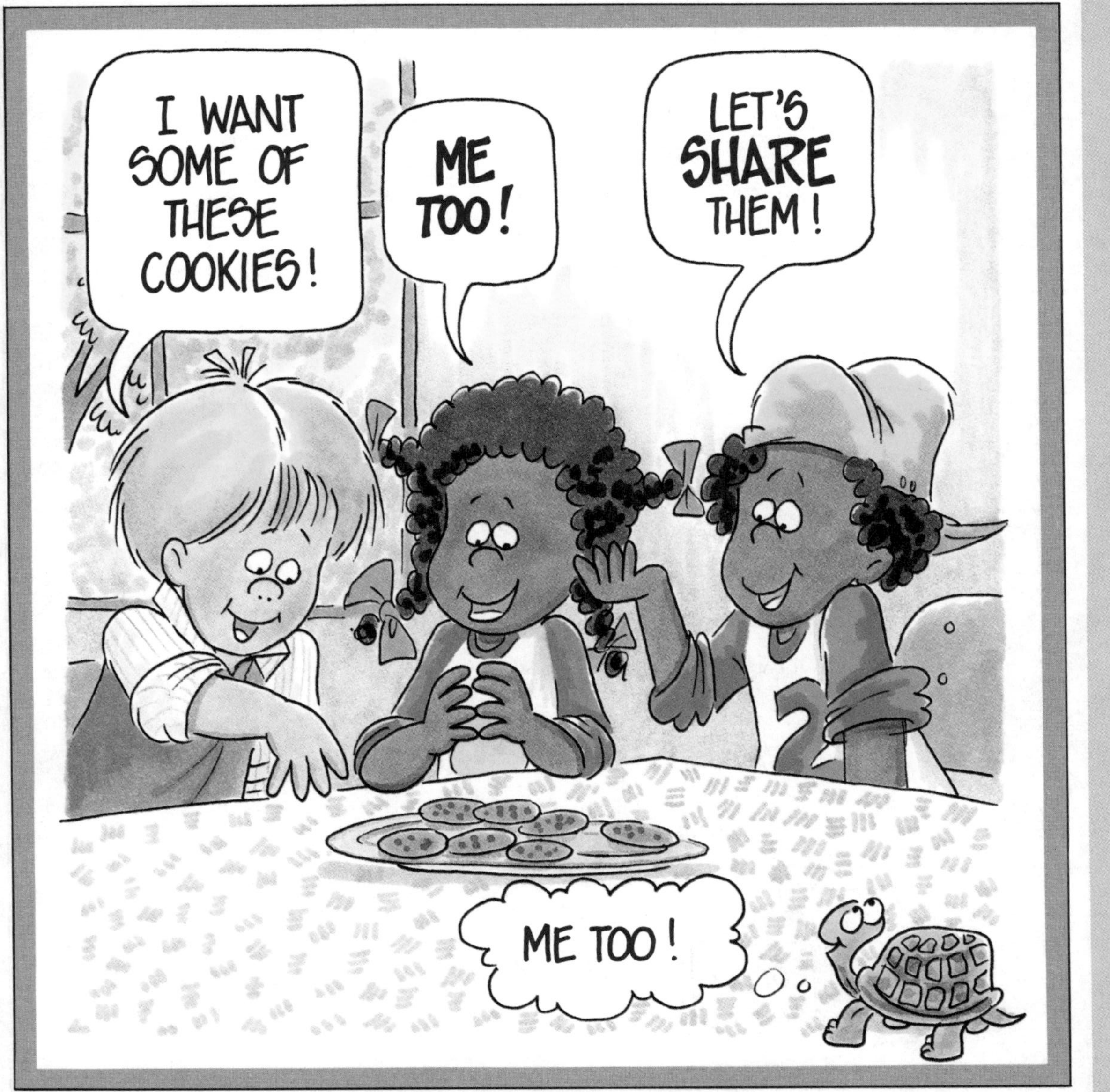
I WANT SOME OF THESE COOKIES!
ME TOO!
LET'S SHARE THEM!
ME TOO!

It is important to be fair when you share. Sharing is fair when every person takes his or her *fair share*.

A *fair share* is the part of something that a person deserves to have.

I'M HUNGRY! I DON'T WANT TO SHARE!
BUT THE COOKIES ARE FOR ALL OF US.
YEAH, EACH OF US SHOULD GET SOME.
THAT'S ONLY FAIR.

Sometimes having a fair share means each person gets the same amount.

WHY DON'T WE EACH TAKE THE SAME NUMBER OF COOKIES?
IT'S FAIR IF WE EACH TAKE TWO COOKIES!
HUMPH!
AND ONE FOR ME.

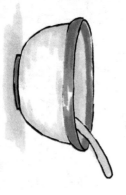

Sometimes a fair share is the amount of something a person really needs. Sometimes a fair share is the amount a person has worked for and earned.

IF WE EACH TAKE TWO COOKIES, THERE WILL BE ONE LEFT OVER! HMMM...
I THINK I SHOULD TAKE THE EXTRA ONE BECAUSE I HELPED BAKE THEM!
THAT'S RIGHT!
WHAT ABOUT ME?

People are being greedy whenever they try to take more than their fair share.

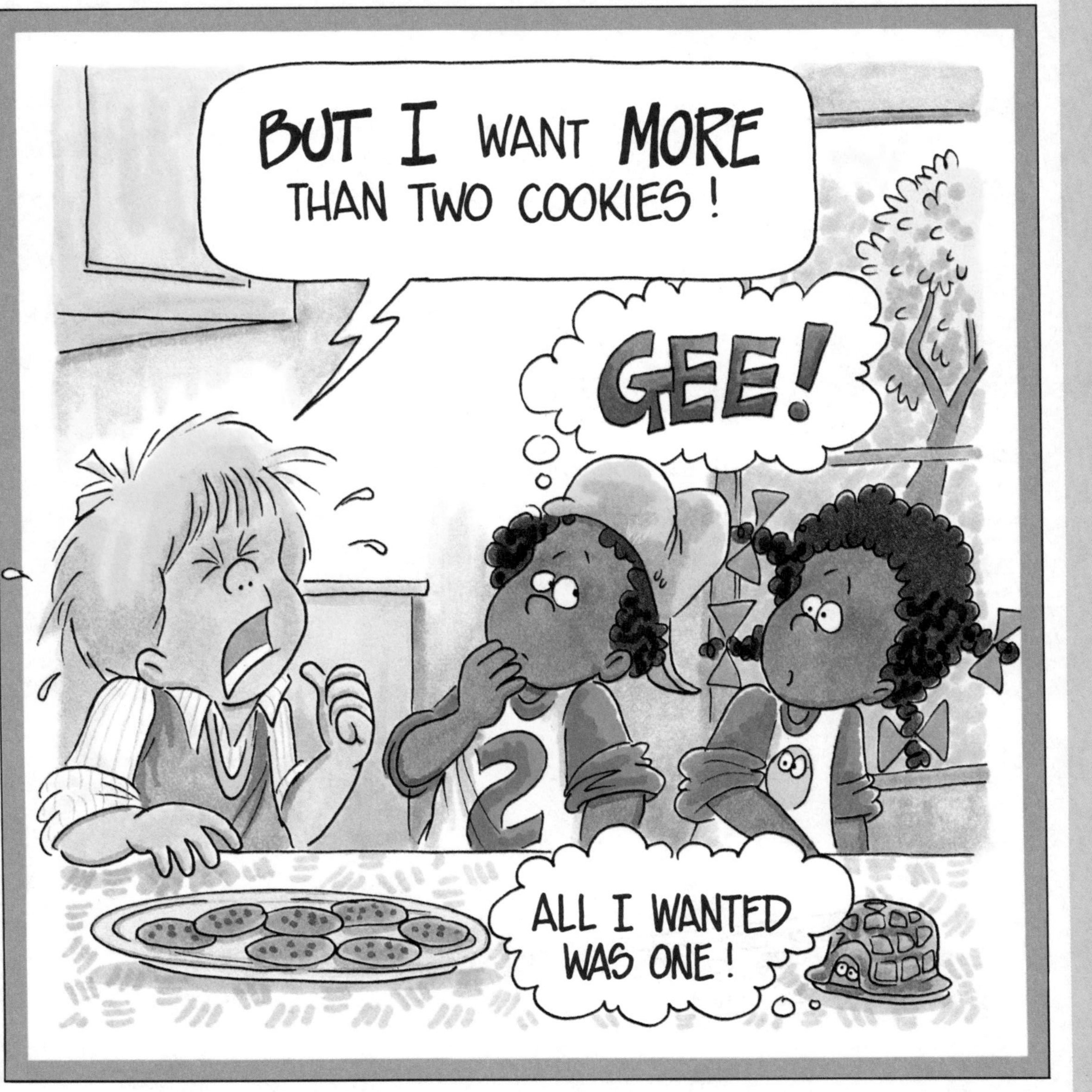
BUT I WANT MORE THAN TWO COOKIES !
GEE!
ALL I WANTED WAS ONE !

Sometimes people are greedy because they *are always dissatisfied.*

They are not happy with what they get.
They always want more.

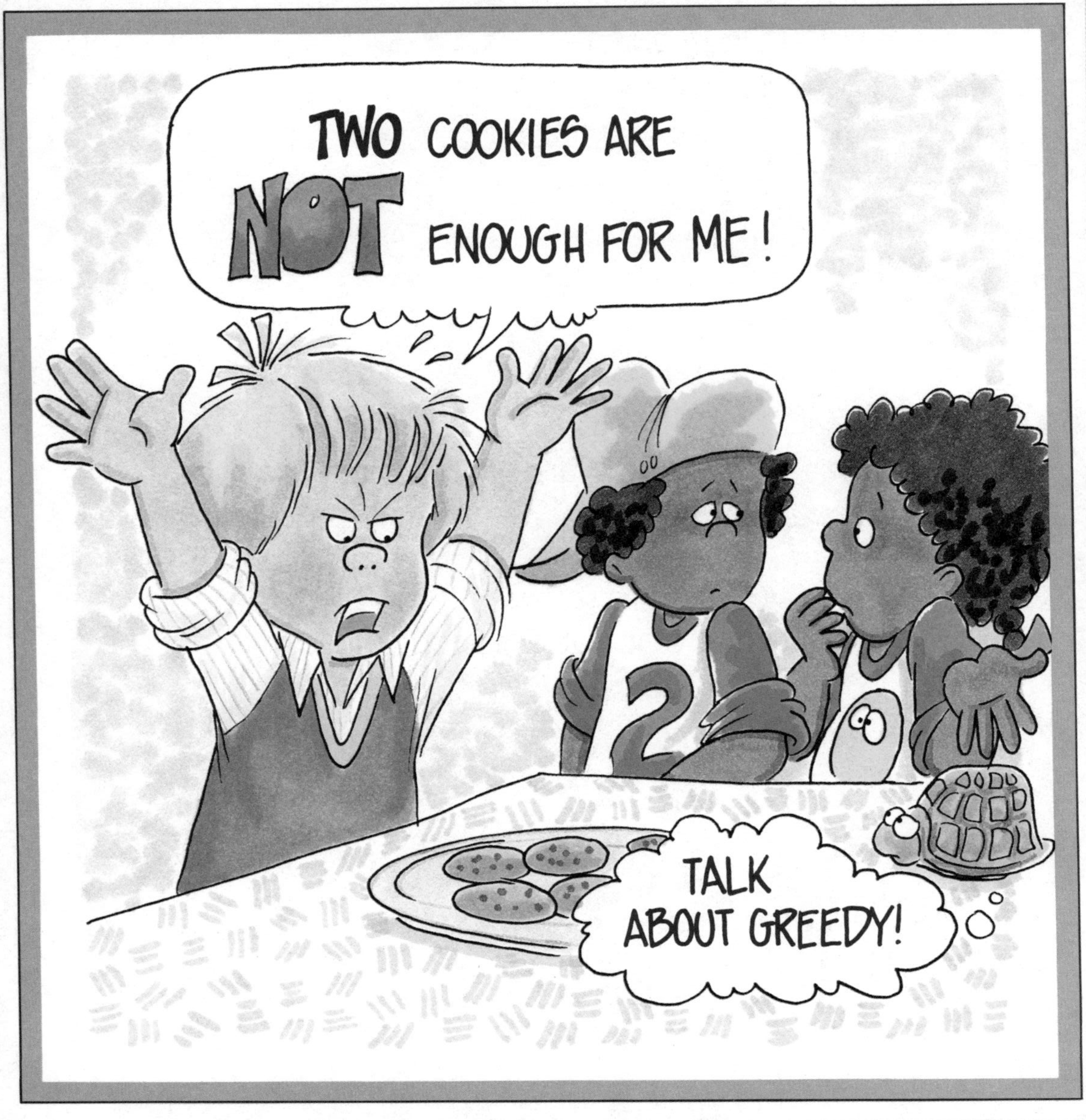
TWO COOKIES ARE NOT ENOUGH FOR ME!
TALK ABOUT GREEDY!

Sometimes people are greedy because they are self-centered.

They care much more about themselves than they care about other people.

BUT WHAT ABOUT US?
WE WANT SOME COOKIES, TOO!
WHO CARES?
I DON'T THINK HE CARES ABOUT ANYBODY BUT HIMSELF.

Sometimes people are greedy because they *feel superior.*

They think they are better than others. They believe they deserve to have more than others.

Sometimes people are greedy because they are unfair.

They do not want others to have a fair share.

It is not fun to be around people who:

- are always dissatisfied,
- are self-centered,
- feel superior, or
- are unfair.

No one likes to be around greedy people.

Greedy people are often unhappy because no one wants to be around them.

Avoid being greedy. Do these things instead:

- Realize that every person deserves a fair share.

- Decide what everyone's fair share will be before you share something.

- Let all the people sharing help decide what a fair share should be.

- Ask your parent or another adult to help you if you and your friends cannot agree on what a fair share should be.

Avoid being greedy. Do these things instead:

- Give other people their fair share before you take yours.
- Be satisfied with your fair share.
- Do not try to take more.
- Do not complain about what you get.

It is important to treat other people the way you want to be treated.

If you do not want other people to be greedy, you must not be greedy.